MOVIN

ANDREW ALDRED

chipmunkapublishing
the mental health publisher

All rights reserved, no part of this publication may be reproduced by any means, electronic, mechanical photocopying, documentary, film or in any other format without prior written permission of the publisher.

>Published by
>Chipmunkapublishing
>United Kingdom

http://www.chipmunkapublishing.com

Copyright © ANDREW ALDRED 2024

Male Rape

If you are a male rape victim
You are more likely to be persecuted.
Then helped by the police.
They stuck me on a Section 48
Because of a crime I had committed years ago
The mental health services went bananas.
Trying to take me in here, there and everywhere.
I had endless hassle trying to deal with them.
But after a few months of jumping through hoops.
They are off my back again and things are normal.
Getting help for a rape case is hard.
Whoever you are and whatever you look like
And whatever your gender and background may be.
For me it was damned near impossible
And probably not worth the effort
I changed my locks and bought a door jammer.

Age of Cruelty

Jane and I went to Matalan recently.
We went to a self-service checkout.
And we were invigilated by the store staff.
She kept giving Jane instructions on what to do.
And Jane wanted to do things in her own time.
We argued with her and finished our shopping.
The goods we had bought were alright.
But the shopping experience was terrible.
We may look a bit rough around the edges.
But shoplifting is not something we do.
And yet we are judged guilty by everyone.
And yes, it does happen in other stores.
This is a result of how other people behave.
And they pick on everyone who walks through the door.
And wonder why they get a bad reaction.
People do not even give you a chance these days.

New Labour

They would have us believe they are honest.
They come on as a lot more conservative than the Tories.
Boasting about being the party for industry and labour
On the basis of some load of bullshit
If you want to see everything, get worse.
Just when the Tories are beginning to turn a corner.
If you want someone irresponsible to spend your money
Then vote for change and new labour.
And in five years the country will be worse than ever
The conservatives deal with industry and money.
They know about these things and what to do with them.
Labour wants to build a national energy company.
Labour wants to scrap oil and gas fields in the sea.
And that will make things more expensive for you and me.
Because it costs more money and will need paying for
Its alright holding the moral high ground.
But when things are impractical and costly it is no good
Keir Starmer shouts the loudest but says nothing.
Just a bunch of ideas and empty rhetoric
A stuffed shirt with very little personality
In an interview he got described as a political robot
I hope when labour get in things do not become worse.

Jewish War Criminal

Everybody gave Benjamin Netanyahu a chance.
To show he could be a reasonable human being.
But he has let those that trusted him down.
And he has shown the world who he really is.
And that is something that a lot of people dislike.
To think that a Jew could contemplate genocide.
After what happened in the holocaust is appalling
Two wrongs never ever made a right.
And Netanyahu is every bit as bad a Hamas.
This is something that can never ever be put right.
It has been bad enough watching it on television.
And my heart goes out to all the innocent people.
This is a catastrophe the world has to sit by and watch.

MOVING ON

Why?

Why does anyone give Donald Trump a chance?
Why do they not just lock him up?
Does he have to prove himself any more guilty?
Of everything he has ever done to be who he is
When will people start to realise, he is rotten?
If you wanted the devil in person, he would be it.
Why does anybody even contemplate voting for him?
He is everything wrong with America and more.
Does anybody really have to be above the law?

The Conservatives

There is only one thing wrong with the Tories.
And that is the foreign policy with the boats.
And that they are going to send people to Rwanda
There has got to be a better way of dealing with the problem.
Displaced people being displaced yet again.
We are no longer part of Europe and want no more refugees.
We want to change the law to suit our purpose.
We are going to tear up the convention on human rights.
To support a cruel and ridiculous policy
It is alright being good with money.
And responsible with the way the country is run.
Scrap this policy and I might vote for you.

Best Show on TV

This show is all about family entertainment.
A number of acts could easily win it.
They have brought people from all over the world.
To compete for the prize on Britain's Got Talent
I have been following it all last week.
I could not pick a winner until the very last act.
They made us howl with laughter and reduced us to tears.
This show makes and breaks people's careers.
They brought us eleven acts that could win the show.
For a prize that is worth a lot more than the money
And the prestige of performing for the King.
It was Sydney Christmas all over again in the final.
The girl who was refused everywhere touched our hearts.
There were two magicians that could have easily won.
And many other people who were champions of their art
Congratulations to Simon Cowell and his team of celebrities.
This show is the only thing I have watched on TV for a while.

Be Careful What You Wish For

There are two elderly men wanting to be president.
One is already a shambling and forgetful wreck.
The other is a sociopathic criminal wanting a reprieve.
Are these two men all we have to run the free world?
Is there really nobody better to do the job?
Does it ever cross their minds they will have to be responsible?
And make some good decisions for the world and the people?
Donald Trump is an isolationist who will pull out of foreign policies.
And he is probably going to win the American election.
What will happen to Ukraine and the Middle East?
It is going to leave a hell of a lot of people in the shit.
And everybody else will have to sort things out without America.
If Trump gets in a hell of a lot of people will hate him
For leaving them in the lurch in their hour of need
And Joe Biden would soon find himself too old for office.
I would see this as a joke if it was not so serious.

Labour Win

The Labour Party has for once got itself in order.
And won an election by a large majority.
And for once they seem to be serious and competent
The country is on its knees, and everything needs fixing.
The prisons, the hospitals, the roads and the schools
And even the houses of parliament for that matter
Somehow the money has to be found for all of this.
And I will be happy if they raise taxes to do it.
I do not mind paying for things if I get a result.
If they will build the infrastructure and do the building
They need the roads, railways and houses to support people.
And now they have got in I hope they sort it out.
They even got my vote and that is saying something.
But to be honest with you there was very little choice.
Labour have won the election, and the hard work starts here.

Synthetic Fuel

They have given electric cars a good chance.

To grab a share of the market and get established.

Every major manufacturer has some electric models.

But I am holding out for the new super fuel.

I still have a petrol car and do not want to change.

And if they can make fuel for it with no emissions, I will use it.

Because I trust the old technology and do not want to change

There are hardly any refuelling points for electric cars in Bolton.

And I do not want to have one at my house.

It is too much expense, and I will have to wait.

Synthetic fuel will become cheaper and solve the problem.

Together for Life

It is seventeen years since our engagement this year.
And although we may not be married any more
We are still lovers and the best of friends.
There is no room for anybody else in our relationship.
We had some friends, but they let us down.
We have had our share of aggravation and illness.
But we simply could not survive without each other.
We are the ying and the yang in every sense.
We have lasted seventeen years and will be together for life.

The Olympics

The Olympics in Paris has lived up to expectations.
The opening ceremony was lavish as they paraded up the Seine.
They had Celine Dion, Lady Gaga and Snoop Dogg in the crowd.
This is a celebration of youth and physical excellence.
However, for every winner there has to be a lot of losers.
There was disruption of the Eurostar line before the event.
Even at the Olympics hatred is never far away.
My best wishes to all the athletes who have entered.
Please remember that it is taking part that counts.
The Olympics has rolled out in 2024. I hope it runs smoothly.

Rock and Roll Dream

I bought a portable recording studio.
To lay down some tracks I had written.
I recently started playing the guitar again.
And suddenly I am where I was fifteen years ago.
I spent last night dreaming about rock and roll.
What might happen to me if I was successful?
I told Jane about my dream the following day.
And she said she needed me to be there for her.
I can mess around with my porta studio at my house.
But playing to an audience is out of the question.
So, I guess I will have to be contented to be a poet.
The only type of musician I will be is a frustrated one.
I suppose I love my girlfriend more than rock and roll.
A rock and roll dream is all it will ever be.

Lung Function Test

I have had a test for my lung function recently.
It is a standard thing for people over the age of 55.
I got the results for it yesterday.
And it showed I have evidence of emphysema.
And a build up a calcium around the heart
I may need to take steroid tablets for my lungs.
And some form of statins to keep my heart working.
The aging process is not easy for anyone.
I booked an appointment to see my doctor.
These are another set of problems I could do without

Gypsy

A man approached me in a car park.

While I sat in my car ready to go

He asked me if I had anything against gypsies.

I declined and he thrust some perfume through the window.

And then he aggressively demanded money for his goods

He had his arms through the window, and I could smell his breath.

I palmed him off with as little as I could give him.

He went on his way, and I drove back to my house.

First there was the homeless, and then aggressive beggars.

And now there are people like him on this car park.

You used to be able to do people a favour, but you cannot anymore.

Heathens

They both look on the other side as subhuman.
They do not see themselves as the heathens they want to kill.
The leaders greet each other as if they were the Pope.
And they all have some deep-rooted belief in religion.
But they want to fight to the death and cannot get on.
They all want total victory, and nobody is prepared to compromise.
Survivors of nuclear war from Hiroshima and Nagasaki
Are worried about the situation in Gaza and Ukraine
And so are a lot of other people including myself.
What will it take for opposing sides to bury the hatchet?
Does there have to be a terrible event to make people stop and think?
When will enough be enough to actually want peace?
Are we all too blinded by hatred to see what we are doing?

Southport

Three little girls from a dancing class are dead.

And people are looking to blame anyone they can.

They want to know if it has anything to do with Islam.

The far right has tried to destroy the local mosque.

Tommy Robinson deserves locking up every bit as much as Zafar Chowdhury

All extremists have a hell of a lot to answer for

Politicians are scoring points out of this situation.

It has been given far too much exposure by the media.

And it all just fuels public anger and outrage.

Of all the places this could happen it is Southport

A town known for its gardening show and a retired population.

The circus comes to town, but it must move on

I hope they can get back to the way things were.

For the families of the little girls, life will never be the same.

Grimley

She has been hanging around for months.
We feed her in Jane's back yard.
She goes up to sit on my lap and be loved.
We bought her an outdoor shelter to use.
We named this strange looking cat Grimley.
She has pierced green eyes and a slight figure.
And she has a peculiar gait with her back feet pointing inwards.
She does not spend all of her time with us.
And we really do not know what to do about her.
But I suppose we are going to feed her at the very least.
We already have a cat and cannot have her inside.
Winter will be challenging for everyone in all sorts of ways.

Far Right Protests

An ex-policeman came on the news to talk about it today.
But he would not condemn the rioters or what they were doing.
Instead choosing to blame the media and the police disclosure.
About the recent crime of a boy who had killed three children
It has come to Bolton and there is a police dispersion order.
I hope I do not get bothered by anyone at my house.
I do not sympathise with the far-right people or the Asians.
I have an African girlfriend and do my best to keep out of trouble.
The government are taking a hard stance on all extremists.
I believe a lot of it is to do with the political party Reform.
I will do my best to live a quiet life and stay out of this shit.
You can lock all the extremists up and throw away the key for me.

ANDREW ALDRED

Live While You Are Young

He wants to join the Navy and be a marine.
He is mad keen on computer games.
And he is trying to get his body in shape.
His parents have not given him the best upbringing.
And he has to rely on the Social Services
To provide his care and put food on the table.
I really hope he succeeds in joining the Navy.
And that he does not die on a military operation
I hope he can take the opportunities that are there?
And get the best out of a difficult life.
Who knows how long any of us will live?
But while you are young you should get out and live

Kamala Harris

She is everything Donald Trump is not.

She is the complete opposite of him.

She is a woman standing for president.

And she has been a high-profile lawyer.

She wants to take Donald Trump to the cleaners.

And I wish her all the luck in the world.

Do you want the free world to be run by a criminal?

Does democracy stand for anything anymore?

She will champion women's rights and those of ethnic minorities.

She will stand up for fairness and equality.

And I hope to God she wins the presidency.

And they put Trump in jail where he belongs.

Toxic Debate

A female Algerian welterweight boxer
Has been on the news a lot recently.
She is a biological woman and is allowed to compete.
At the Olympics where she has won a gold medal
Everyone seems to want to have a go at her.
Because she is in a different league to the others
She satisfies the rules and is in no way transgender.
She is a legitimate sportswoman and a good one.
She has had to learn and has lost fights.
JK Rowling, Donald Trump and Elon Musk have called her out.
For supposedly being a man which she is not
She might not be the sort of woman these people like
But I wish they could all bottle their opinions.
She is taking them to court to sue them.
And I hope she takes some of their money off them.

Doxing

I was looking through my catalogue of books.

On the internet when I noticed a poem

It was supposedly by me, but it was not one of mine

It was on a website called All Poetry, so I read it.

It seemed to be reaching out to me through the ether.

The writer of it seemed to be talking to me.

I suppose I should take it as some form of flattery.

I only hope not everyone wants to steal my name.

And write strange poems on the internet in the future.

Another Sleepless Night

I tried to go to bed but could not.

I got in and rested my head on the pillow.

But I would be damned if I could sleep.

I copied some songs from a record on my guitar.

Wrote the lyrics and practised the riffs.

One was by Reo Speedwagon, the other by BTO.

I wrote a couple of poems of which this was the latter.

It is six o clock in the morning and still no sleep.

It is just as well I normally do better than this.

Jane needs me at her house while she gets work done.

For the next couple of days and this is all I need

To get ready for some time on my toes

Another sleepless night. Well, that's just the way it goes.

Responsible Prime Minister

They said on Loose Women he lacked charisma.
And they preferred Boris Johnson for his rhetoric.
Boris talked the talk but was incompetent.
Keir Starmer does by and large what I want him to do.
There are no great speeches or radical moves.
We are reaching out to Europe for help and solidarity.
They are solving the problem with the overcrowded prisons.
And yes, a lot of people do not belong there.
We know they are going to raise some taxes.
To get the money they need to fix the country.
Do not forget it was the conservatives who left it like this.
And there is a huge shortfall of money to make up.
I believe Rachel Reeves and Keir Starmer deserve a chance.

The Loft

Jane got her loft boarded out.
And I cleaned the broken cladding away.
Put it in bags and carried it down the ladder.
I took away lots of broken bits of wood.
Then I mended the brickwork around the beams
One of which had cracked and been left.
It had another beam beside it to do its job.
And they really should have flagged it up.
When they did the roof earlier in the year
But it is holding its own weight.
And it will have to stay until they do the roof again.
If it is moved it risks dislodging the tiles
It will last Jane out and be a burden to someone else.
I had all sorts of plans to fix it.
But it is safer not being moved or mended.

Car Park Incident

I was parking my car in an awkward space.

And reversed out again to get my car straight.

And collided with a white Toyota, also reversing.

I straightened my car up and got out of it.

And was faced by a young Asian man with a beard.

I apologised to him, and he said he would phone his Aunty.

We went to do our shopping, and he was there when we came back.

And so were his Aunty and Uncle who had appeared out of nowhere.

They badgered me for my insurance details.

And they wanted me to take responsibility for the incident.

I said that I was not entirely to blame.

And pointed out that both vehicles were reversing.

I said that I would admit liability for my part of the incident.

And that I was getting in my car and leaving

I submitted a report and some photographs to my insurers.

And I only hope they do not try and blame me.

For an accident that was not entirely my fault

Feeling Hated

I went to the chemist to get my girlfriends prescription.//
And I had to wait for half an hour.//
And then they said they had lost the prescription//
And that they would have to check the order manually//
Ten minutes later I was out of Asda.//
And went home to find a dead tree in my front yard.//
So, I put it over the fence into the back yard.//
And went round to saw it up and put it in the bin.//
All this on top of a recent incident at a car park//
And waiting for deliveries that have not come.//
Everything seems to be all to cock today.//
Everybody seems to hate me and put obstacles in my way.

Busy Week

It is the end of a busy week with plenty to do.
I have filled her newly boarded attic with things from downstairs.
I took empty boxes up and filled them with bags of stuff.
So as not to put too much pressure on her new ladder
I painted my fence at the front and sprayed it at the back.
Somehow getting it all done in a couple of days
I had a blood test for the tablets I am taking for my heart.
And I mowed the grass in my front and back garden.
I am tired and stressed and need to relax and sleep.
You can bet your bottom dollar it's been a busy week.

Buying Free Speech

There are those that think you can buy free speech.
That because they have more money, we should listen to them.
Well, everyone has a voice, and we are all equal in Gods eyes.
I might go on Elon Musk's platform if I thought it was worth the money.
And I agreed with anything that was being said on it.
The rich boys think they are unaccountable and can do what they want.
But Andrew Tate, Donald Trump, Elon Musk and the rest of them
Do not realise the amount of people they offend every day.
By whom they are and the fact that they exist at all
You might think I fall into the same category for different reasons.
But I have a lot less to lose and have already been where they are going.
You can buy free speech, but it is not worth anything if you have nothing worth saying.

It is Never Enough

There is the Post Office scandal and the payments.
The people living in buildings with dangerous cladding.
The compensation for the infected blood scandal
The cost of living is rising, and wages will not keep up.
The doctors, nurses and rail workers want more money.
Successive governments have borrowed more than they should.
The pandemic and the war in Ukraine have cost us money.
The population is living longer and requires care in old age.
There is the cost of climate change and clean energy.
It all needs paying for and there is not enough money.
The workmen that come round to my house are looking.
For anything they can do to get more money out of me
But my pockets are not that large, and I have to survive.
People are going to have to make do with less and get on.
But everybody wants a holiday and a new car with alloy wheels.
And they cannot understand why they cannot have these things.
When that is the shit the media feed us every day
The people of this country are going to have to pay for a better life.
By working hard, making their money last and going without
We are going to have to get by and make what we have enough for us.

Do Not Make the Bear Angry

The European and American leaders are talking.
About the latest development to the war in Ukraine
The Ukrainians want long range missiles to attack Russia.
And I would urge the greatest caution in making this decision.
Vladimir Putin says he will take appropriate action but will not commit further.
And this might mean a full-scale war in Europe.
The Russians have already threatened to obliterate London.
And they could do with one well-placed nuclear bomb.
Never mind what is right and wrong, how far can we push them.
Before they retaliate in a decisive way, and we are done for.
The Americans are a safe distance away, but we are not.
North Korea, Iran and China are in the background.
And we had better be very bloody careful about what we do.
The Ukrainians need to get the Russians out of their country.
And maybe we need to work towards that instead of all-out war.
The Russian bear will get increasingly angry, and we will not be forgiven.

Huw Edwards

This was an intelligent man who knew what he was doing.
All the evidence on show was a few WhatsApp messages.
And when WhatsApp is untraceable why is it in existence?
Everybody uses it because they know nothing will come back to them.
From cheating husbands and housewives to people like Huw Edwards
He said he liked the pictures a convicted paedophile sent him.
But when he was prompted to buy more which were described as illegal
He realised what he was getting into and refused to go further.
And yes, he probably has something wrong with him mentally.
A lot of paedophiles do, and the country's mental hospitals are full of them.
But Huw Edwards will not go to prison, instead being placed on probation.
And having to sign a sex offenders register for the next seven years.
This is what money, and a decent lawyer can do for you.
But nobody can bring back his reputation and social standing for him.
He will forever be a disgrace to everybody he came into contact with

The Warmest August

Sea levels are rising as the ice caps melt.

It seems all we can do is sit by and watch.

We cannot change society rapidly enough.

To affect the climate of our planet to any degree

We know the climate fluctuates periodically.

It will go warmer and then go colder.

The fish will die, and the food chain will alter.

Nature will die in future years in the Arctic.

The rains have come down over central Europe.

Poland and Czechoslovakia have had huge floods.

While fires go on in Portugal and tidal waves in China

We can only hope that nature will correct itself.

That we may be saved, and the weather will stabilise.

This planet is getting harder to live in for all forms of life.

Dirty War

Israel has sunk to a new low in the War.
They have managed to take out most of Hezbollah.
By blowing up the pagers they had in their pockets
This ideology really is taking terror to the terrorists.
This is like the script of some bizarre movie.
And you wonder what the hell they are going to do next.
I am seeing internet devices in a different light as well.
My phone, my computer or anything else could be armed.
What does this mean for the war in Gaza and Lebanon?
God knows, but I do not think any good will come of it.
This war started out as rape and mutilation of women and children.
And has progressed by reducing a whole nation to rubble.
With many thousands of people left in a hopeless situation
And this is just the latest unconventional chapter in this war.
When are we going to see any humanity in all of this?
I think a lot more people will be dead before that happens.

ANDREW ALDRED

Broken Britain

We have a police force that does not know right from wrong.
A mental health service that is prepared to do anything
To sweep the evidence of serious crimes under the carpet
A government that is self-serving and will do anything to keep in power.
A workforce that just wants to draw a wage and do nothing.
Labour's slogan was Change but I do not see anything happening.
Everyone seems to think they are a gangster and can do what the hell they want.
Because that is what is on TV and all they aspire to
And we are all trying to carry on with this madness.
I do not know whether to despair or laugh out loud.
But somewhere along the line we ought to accept we are all crazy

Malicious Software

I experienced my own problems with the Post Office software today.
An item I had ordered from Amazon on 21st September.
Was listed as having been delivered the previous July.
The tracking for it was unavailable on the Post Office site.
Many people's lives have been ruined by the company's faulty software.
I know something about computers having passed an HND in 1992
And I will tell you that the programmers and systems analysts.
Employed by the company are to blame for the scandal.
While they blame the people in charge, they go unnoticed.
They are still in their jobs because they are needed for their skills.
They are not easily replaceable and so are not accountable.
Software is only as good as the people who create it.
And if they get everything wrong it is bound to malfunction
It is alright blaming bosses, politicians and the company's hierarchy.
But the people who designed and built Horizon are the real culprits.

Insane

The Israeli prime minister and war cabinet want their heads testing.
They want to drag us all into Netanyahu's holy war.
In Britain we are beginning to distance ourselves from them
And I really would love it if America would step back as well.
If they did not have the weapons, they could not have the war.
And the middle east could get on with living in peace once again.
But the terrorists will not give up and do not know they are beaten.
And Israel seems intent on levelling the entire region.
The people in charge of both sides are absolutely crazy.
It takes two to start a fight but then things get right out of hand.
People want revenge and vindication, and it never ends.
Until one side is well beaten and has had to surrender
Everyone thinks they can make things better by making them worse.
When its all over it does not matter who was right and who was wrong
God is forever on the side of the big battalions, and they are always right.

Age is Just a Number?

Mike Tyson says he is fighting Jake Paul to show that age is just a number.
I have always thought he was doing it just for the money he will earn.
To be able to have a final payday and retire for good.
Age is just a number, but it does not get any smaller as time goes on.
You get less able mentally and physically. You have to adapt.
You get a different job or progress up the company ladder.
You have to be desperate to fight a man half your age to earn some money.
People become disabled and have to think again about what they are doing.
This is why there will always be a welfare state for those that need it.
It is a pity a lot of people drawing benefits in this country should also be working.
Age should not necessarily stop you from doing anything you want to
But please be sensible and realise people get killed in all sorts of situations.
If you put your mind and body on the line continuously it will let you down
Age is just a number, but it never gets any less as time goes on.
Never mind what you do to stay fit and look good. Age will catch up with you.

ANDREW ALDRED

Backed Into a Corner

Ukraine has had no choice from day one.
They always had their backs against the wall.
And have had to fight for their country and freedom.
And sooner or later their allies will have to commit.
If Russia does not retreat and lose face
Israel is taking on all terrorist Arab states.
And was never going to hold back on the holy war.
The other players in the game have disguised their hands.
And operated from the sidelines staying out of trouble.
All of a sudden Iran has pitched in and bombed Israel.
And that could mean a lot of people lining up for a fight.
America has long been an enemy of Iran and could get involved.
Iran has been supplying Russia with weapons from afar.
The same as Europe and America have done for Ukraine.
Iran has said Israel will be punished for its actions.
And this could be the start of a very ugly scene.
Sooner or later, we will all have to take responsibility.
And we will either sort this situation out or fight.
Israel has dug a hole it will not get out of easily.
Ukraine has always been fighting for its life and existence.
Nobody will compromise and there is only victory or defeat.
We are all backed into a corner and will have to fight our way out.

Outdated

Donald Trump's foreign policies have been superseded.

It is no longer possible to sleep with the devil for economic advantage.

The days when America could be friends with Putin and North Korea are gone.

There will no longer be able to be any peace with Iran.

Trump's foreign policy is not what America wants at the moment.

And it is crucial for America and the rest of the world he does not get voted in

There is a job to do on the world stage and he is not the man to do it.

It will take more than a crooked businessman to fix the world's problems.

Never mind abortion, women's rights and all the rest of it

If America wants a free world Kamala Harris is the only choice

Desensitized

The kids today are numb to everything.
By the time they have reached ten years old
They learn not to give a shit off their parents.
And we all wonder why we have teenage murderers.
Little Johnny could have learned a trade.
But he was too busy playing call of duty.
And that was all he wanted to do in adult life.
That was how he felt, and it was right for him.
I was just the same when I was young.
My mother cried, my father shook my hand, and I joined up.
And it gave me some sort of life before I left.
Physically and mentally disabled for the rest of my days.
It seemed to me to be the best option at the time.
And at least I have a pension to see my life out.
You very rarely get your life back after a bad start.
And we all need to do the best we can for our kids.
To make sure they manage to reach a decent age.
Before they are too old and ill to do anything productive
Does life have to be so bloody hard for everyone?
We had all better learn to start caring about something.
And not be blind and desensitised to what is going on.

Build

In Bolton we are building our way out of a crisis

There are new housing developments in Farnworth and Bolton

The area has been under construction for five years.

And now things are starting to get completed.

The finishing touches to a lot of projects are happening.

And there will be new affordable housing for a lot of people.

Maybe we can be something other than a ghost town again.

Maybe we can be the city we always wanted to be.

With a winning football team and some decent jobs

I will be so glad when all the work is finished.

And the council can spend money on something other than construction.

Somehow this dirty old town will be back on its feet.

And people will be able to take a pride in the place they live in

The Opt-Out Clause

I cannot name one ideology that I believe in
There is something fundamentally wrong with all of them.
I do not believe in any religion or political persuasion.
I do not believe that any colour or creed is better than another.
All I can see is a world pulled apart by opinionated people.
So, I will tell you you're all full of shit and had better learn to get on.
I am getting old and disillusioned with the rest of you.
I no longer want to work for anyone and am not able to
I have nothing to offer anyone that is worth having.
Apart from to the few people I know and still have contact with
I love my ex-wife, and we will remain together as long as we can.
It is down to everyone else to find their own way in this life.
I do not believe in the community and will be opting out of everything.
Apart from giving money to the few charities I do support.
What did anyone ever want to steal an old man's body for anyway?
It's a mad world and all I can do is let it keep turning.
Whilst I get my feet up and drink my next cup of tea
The opt-out clause is the only one that is left for me.

The Rat Race

We are all kept frantically running in the rat race.

They make you think you need everything they have to sell.

So, you work sixty hours a week to buy it all.

They keep you in debt so you can be exploited.

Whilst the cost of everything goes forever up

They promote gambling to take your hard-earned money away.

They sell you drink, drugs and sex to make you ill.

And we all keep running full pelt until we collapse.

They give you religion to berate yourself with

They give you a government you are responsible for

And everything continually wears you down to nothing.

Whoever you are once you are dead you are soon forgotten.

And everything you worked for is soon swallowed up.

It is a consumer society full of scavengers and rats.

And everything about it and in it will chew you up.

Milton Keynes UK
Ingram Content Group UK Ltd.
UKHW030655101124
450942UK00001B/9